Wailing on Whisper Street

by Bree Bailey

Write Bloody Publishing

writebloody.com

First edition.
ISBN: 978-1949342536

Cover Design by Derrick C. Brown
Interior Layout by Nikki Steele
Edited by Wess Mongo Jolley
Proofread by Adrian Wyatt
Author Photo by Jilisa Bellachhab

Type set in Bergamo.

Write Bloody Publishing
Los Angeles, CA

Support Independent Presses
writebloody.com

Wailing on Whisper Street

Wailing on Whisper Street

You can achieve
your wildest
dreams -
I'm rooting for you.
Always.
Bree ♡

Message To God or Alanis Morissette. They're the Same, Right?

In the damp abyss of the room,
where mold drifts up to the ceiling,

I plunge forward into the ancient
vibrato of elder shipwrecks rocking.

The husk of the horizon says, 'Be hopeful,'
as I descend into the squid-inked floor.

There are no wings or jewels for angels who
martyr rescue in the deep ends of New Jersey.

No verse is apt to heal a hurricane in heaven,
funeral at a wedding, or some flurry of folly.

How I float resides in the stream of my scream,
and no, I will not die.

These stories I've swum will not die.
I owe everything I have to the angels.

A(wo)men.

Growing Up

Growing up is… my brother was killed by his new roommates once my family shut their doors / like an alligator ripping my throat and bashing my bleeding face against Floridian asphalt / Oh wait, that was my brother / like the end-of-the-month bills and hoping it was the first of the month full of groceries and a fridge made of no one's fault / like Section 8 Housing / like *Dios te bendiga* after someone too young dies / like a snowstorm that doesn't let me bury my father in gentle ground / snowstorm that doesn't let me brownbag an avalanche of cloaked alcoholism / like running / like shrugging off therapy / like the violence of a bellyache / like brunch mimosas and me at the bottom, less / like marrying a feminist who becomes silent when his frat brothers make rape jokes / like punchlines and hemlines bursting and truth's pounding despair / like realizing I am not dead yet / like knowing authenticity is better than faking the smile / full-figured with six figures / book deals / like sending care packages with hand-drawn cards / like boot scoot keychains that say *San Antonio* / like gold foil starry stickers on letters to my aunt's sick dog / like finally saying the word therapy / like finally affording therapy / finally affording to be honest in therapy / like *Cheers! We made it, Chingonas* / like realizing mama's breath isn't a flower but would be the most beautiful / like gratitude for my siblings' growth and fresh roots / like *Arriba, abajo, por el centro, por el dentro* / like coming clean in the 2am calls / like celebrating a mundane Sunday because mourning always comes / like screaming lyrics at the top of my lungs / a good mid-afternoon fuck / like *Lo siento* / I forgive them / I forgive you / like a phoenix hiccupping laughter crumb ashes / like a reader's entertainment and my truth / like, let's be honest.

Ode to the Day I Grew Boobs

The photographer's greasy thumb grazes his peppercorn-
black goatee as his lips smack joy at his joke,
unbothered by my fourth-grade class' discomfort.
Lingering in the last row, my ponytail sheens of glitter
and butterfly clips, nothing like the tween shimmer
of Rose and Carolina. They are front-row dainty
training bra beauties. The lens spotlights their formation.
My chest heaves feeling when false exposure clicks.
Having boobs is not like the Baywatch lifeguards make it seem.
A speckled fly dances atop Ms. Haynes' blue coffee mug.
It becomes an unnoticed, stealthy little shit; my hero.
My chest, too large, aches for less weight so close to my heart.
Take yesterday, when Ms. Haynes sent a note home,
and I never had anything but straight A's sent home,
so this tiny grey envelope was sludgewater making me sick.
I held the envelope to the microwave light, anxiety helping none.
Dismayed and green, I handed the note to my mom.
She remained mouse-silent until three hours later.
Tossing me a faded Kathy Ireland brand bra,
brittle words fell from her mouth:
'You see, you're becoming a woman.
Use this now until I can get you something that fits better.'
I'd wear the yellow fabric like a name tag with an ugly middle
name for the next two weeks.
The mix of Brillo and White Diamonds sweat-cloaked
the nylon giving its whiff an added uplift.
Months passed by before I found the note with my photo in a drawer.
In flowy, black-inked script, the note read:
'Older boys are staring and this needs to be fixed fast.'
This decree to 'fix' a problem with a body that knew no wrong,
became a painfirst grasp of the space we allow an hourglass to hold.
Wings over my chest, I rest, a deflated mosquito in the last row.
Over the next few years, I'd tremble when any man hollered
'Say cheese, sweetheart!' and Brillo stale perfume shrouded me unclean.

Admission of My Most Expensive Fault

double broken golden shovel with lines from Hanif Abdurraqib

How my ear nerves amplify what isn't
small, gather speech in my throat. What of it?
We've left our native home, grown grim and funny,
become empty brownstone-stooped dollars. How,
because loss haunts us, there's a splintered silence
of chronic poverty. Yet, I plump with cash. Can
all rich distractions erase ache? Undress
these charmeuse desires, weak charlatan. Split two
things from the safe I hold. What of boxes and bodies?

Forgive Me, Father.

I have only lived with failed conjugation,

born of two abandoned souls that
exchanged me, a no-longer-virgin body,

in the absence of God.

Margaret

after Sheleen McElhinney

My mother is the greyest day in April.
She survives as a Blarney stone found in Belleville.
I nicknamed her 'Southern Transplanted Jesus.'
She keeps folded bills tucked in a faded grey Bible,
at the unwound nape of 'Sister Rosetta' tapes,
both heirlooms of her womanly wealth.
Not a radio, but my mother is a singing suitcase
of well-versed grief, full of local obituaries
with her name and role next to every spirit she loved.
She is a holy voyeur reading *The Star-Ledger,*
not for names she recognizes, but for the unified poetry
of something constant for her prayers.
Obituaries to store with her baggage.
Welcomer of tragedy, compassionate
Mother Teresa of Jacksonville.
Her penance paid whenever she forgave
me at my drunk and stumbliest. Long before I made
sestinas in her honor, she washed my period-
soaked bed sheets of rebellion.
Dressed in the wrinkled trauma of her own world wars,
Sweet Mama Maggie wore my regrets as hand-me-downs
in reverse disaster. My mother saved every penny, locked
every door, and bargained twice with God before closing her eyes
each night.
For years, she rose early to buy new-to-me shoes, underwear,
and push-up bras to shield me from the complications of being
the muse behind The Commandments.
She is angelic grace sprung forward
in loud, living, freckled flesh,
like thunderclaps celebrating a cloud's homecoming,
unlike me — agnostic, alone, and weeping in church on Easter.

La Princesa de Macy's

When autumn leaves begin crunching outside the doorways, I flinch
when I overhear the eighth-grade boys approach,
teasing me about clothes.

The cafeteria's french-fry-caked linoleum tiles give me no cover
when they call me a princess and point at my SNAP bologna sandwich.

Antonio and Erik, peas in pods of dumb and dull who can barely
spell 'bologna' right, ask: *'Why do you have a fancy sweater,
but eat free lunch?'*

'What happened to your chariot and crown, smelly Princesa?'
Julieta, my prima on my dad's side, tells me

I shouldn't listen to the mean frog-voiced boys.
'They're jealous of how smart you are and that you'll get outta here,'

Juli says on Saturday morning when we head to the Goodwill.
Juli calls the Goodwill "Macy's." Flowing from

lip-glossed Boricuan lips, the store name sambas
to life as we ride the bus down Broadway.

Julieta doesn't receive welfare like my family.
She has two jobs with benefits and a rich boyfriend

that put a white baby in her belly.
My mother, in a manner that says she longs to be

a grandma one day, greedily accepts Juli's invitation
to go shopping for baby clothes. I go another way.

I head to the clearance rack to fetch a sparkly Michael Kors
sweater and feel the cloth surge the glamor in my skin.

I could look 'designer' after a week of not eating.
Juli shouts through pearly Chiclets what becomes my favorite song:

*¡Qué bella! Dios! La Princesa de Macy's!
Look, Maggie! Your baby's a princess!*

Oldest Brother

Ice cream trucks depress me. First dates become somber melodies, too. What can I say? My prowling dread claws my brain like a haunting symphony. On the spot, I can never tell you my favorite ice cream flavor or how many siblings I have. My oldest brother, Junior, drove an ice cream truck, believe it or not, and delivered frozen luck with gumball eyes to anyone from cul-de-sacs to trailer parks along Collins Road for three summers. Crumpled dollars went to gas to fill the tank and rainbow sprinkles, hoping to spread something bright and allow kids to forget beatings from earlier nights. Everyone was worth a million bucks, so no one had to pay. Four months into Junior's twenty-sixth year and the summer of my eleventh birthday, he got roommates and bought his own truck. He washed it weekly with blue-collar sweat, stocked it up with Costco-bought sweetness, and made a promise to let me eat everything I wanted when I heard his tune next. My belly would ache with how much he loved me. Full of promise and calories, I stopped eating dessert waiting for his song to enter my stomach. One week would pass before the men he shared a home with left his body idly in a ditch outside my cousin Renee's trailer park. Like abandoned ice cream, his skin melted in the hot Florida sun. As the last of him pooled around his killers' feet, they searched his wallet, hoping for cash, crack, and a way out, only to find sprinkles stuck to my school picture. They left it behind, not having teeth sweet enough to face little sisters until the law said they had to. I would stop eating altogether without notice until an ice cream truck barreled down my street four weeks later and I collapsed barefoot, sobbing in the street like a bent spoon. All to say, I think it's vanilla. I think my love for my three siblings, like my ice cream flavor all summed up, is plain vanilla. Do you believe me, and will there be a second date?

Hormones and Clapton During First Period

Time can bring you down / Time can bend your knees / Time can break your heart / Have you begging please / Begging please / Beyond the door / There's peace, I'm sure
—"Tears in Heaven," Eric Clapton

Junior year of high school is when my English teacher is
the hottest preppy punk my class has ever seen.
At sixteen, in Advanced Poetry,
everything we learn is about love and
heartbreak. I'm not wrong,
but I'm not right either.

With a blood-red focus, I fear the
stain of my period if I should need to stand to
pass out papers, so I look how I feel: down.
It's creative writing day, my favorite.

My teacher says he created a playlist
to get our juices flowing.
We all thirst without needing any help.
The first song is by Hall & Oates.
We scribble like gleeful squirrels,
delirious on dreams come true.

Next up, a ballad.
Things are getting serious as LeAnn Rimes
tells us she can't live without someone.
I'd be lost if I lost you.
Rhyming comes easy in moments like these.
Blue, true, glue.
I can stay on this page – I never need to leave.

Suddenly, mid-rhyme,
a song comes on and I
have to find an exit.
Eric Clapton sings of the strength to endure,
and all I want to do is be carried away.
Period woes, be damned.

This song isn't a song; it's a reminder
of my brother's blood still rich in
the gravel pit of our unshakeable loss.
When we went to place flowers at the scene,
three months fresh after my brother's murder,
my uncle remarked while lighting a Newport,
"Wow. All that brown right here is dried blood.
You ever see this much brown before?
I sure haven't."

On the side of an isolated Southern road,
my brother's life became a puddle of *Tears in Heaven.*
It pooled between the toes of a little sister's sandals
as she watched her mother collapse into the brownest of all dirt.
And years later, she would burst from a room full of teenagers,
a siren, all brilliant and crimson, and the boys all think,
"Guess it must be her time of the month."

She Could Be Martha

Like a bad hangover, a hostage held in my brain,
it's been a year since my brother's been gone.
My mom is in her late forties but looks fifty.
The pills bulldozed between her lips help in achieving this.

We're playing a game we learned from her medications,
the ones the US government gives her for free
from a psychiatrist that it also gives her for free.
We all end up paying for what this land of the free gives us.

The doctor prescribes daily Medicaid mind-bending blends,
rather than smaller, more frequent doses of organic kindness.
The psychiatrist doesn't ask her how she's feeling when she visits,
but rather, *Why are you here again?*

He can't spell her name; at every appointment, she gets a new one.
Today, her name is "Martha."
He knows her twenty-six-year-old son
was murdered by his roommates
and that she hasn't slept in six days.

He knows the prescription of psychoactives has stopped her
from scaring the nurses with her tears each visit
and that's good enough for him.
Happier nurses make his job easier.

Please, he begs, *make my job easier.*

So maybe being poor didn't cause her brain to chemically rot.
But if you asked me what I wished for on my twelfth birthday
in between her gasping cries behind closed doors,
it wasn't to resurrect my angel of a brother.

No. My wish was for my mom to get a better psychiatrist.
And although the doctor couldn't spell my mother's name right,
I can still spell his.

Through the fuzz and static that comes of my brain,
he is forever cemented as captive.

Freebird

"Does your conscience bother you? Tell the truth."
— "Sweet Home Alabama," Lynyrd Skynyrd

The final moments of a plane crash
are not as gruesome as folks believe.

Most of the already-dying die from the explosion,
if not hypoxia — the act of oxygen becoming

a reverse and determined suction cup.
Scooped up in supernatural hands, all gelatin-

bodied humans with sins diddle-daddling on display,
wishing their departure came sooner rather than on time.

The naval dropout held me in jealous chapped hands
during a four-month Casanova summer.

My fool's hand played at first dates, fawning over his brood
while a noose hung around his commitment finger.

He was a boy interested in flying high above grim
reaping after finding his daddy dead in a basement.

He told me his sergeants nicknamed him 'Ghost' when they
took roll. Damage dancing can be more sexual than a good fuck.

So of course, I grabbed him by his tragedy, placed it on my ass,
and grinded to the awful Skynyrd song.

I shared lies for drugs and told him dying doesn't scare me and
I lost my brother before the world had the enormity of 9/11.

That was enough to keep me scared of flying.
He peered, in an obscene James Dean way,

and blew his Cuban-to-him, cheater-to-me cigar smoke my way,
You're high and dead right now.
I was. And I felt so low and alive.

And that's when I knew that the captain always burns in the crash.
Searing and superficial — scorching every memory, kidney,
pancreas, toe,

fingernail, steel — Earth — until every morsel of the good green
mother is caped in
brutal sacrificial black — the propeller, the luggage — the broken
records at dive

bars being played about broken people loving broken people
who are no longer in the same broken place.

He said 9/11 made him enlist and Ronnie Van Zant,
a hometown hero, provided our skylark soundtrack.

I became a jaded jet, aching for his unrefined gasoline.
We laughed and fucked to see a day until we didn't.

'Cause our love, like those country roads that raised those boys to
play those songs,
were the same that grew to separate them, to take flight, to depart,
to burst.

Otro Nombre

after Danez Smith

junkyard Jezebel of Jacksonville
one man's rib and another's ripened ruin
goddess of ill-gotten grief
vacant rental of maternal estate
poster parent of craven desire
pregnant drowning mermaid
bubbly enough to sting sorrow
one shot of tequila starlight sunrise
smeared red peesticks of possibilities
supernova of stories of who I used to be
aborted planet, Pluto-eyed pirate
bruised seedless orange outside abandoned clinic
postpartum anatomy made of wilted citrus womb
gentle badgirl gospel who grew to frighten the faith
sweet choir girl stuck in the throat of a toilet
I stapled a cross over my lips, is that another name for salvation?

I Eat Sad Peanut Butter, the Fat-Free Kind

and become everything blogs warned me about.
Served on a plate of melancholic allergens,
sad-girl-soft buttery reflection stares back.
I am every sad-girl, ad-girl, sad.

Avoid eye contact with me. I'll make your orbs
crawl out of your head. Peanut butter cup hips
with not-quite white chocolate breasts.
What am I?

Don't make me moisten my lips
in delight.
Trust me —
and these hands?
Built soft and tender with tissue paper

I managed to stuff in even when I had the biggest tits
in all the eighth grade.
Jenny down my block who works at the hair shop
says size matters.

Bigger is *always* better.
Why would anyone lie about that?

I make myself desirable in all the wrong ways,
Expand or deflate to satisfy any peculiar palette

as I line myself in coke, strobe lights, and
bottles of daddy issues called Not Your Father's.

I can't remember.
What was I saying?

Do you believe in the zodiac? I'm a Cancer.
I'll eat you alive, you're delicious.

Ode to Amy Coney Barrett Driving Me to the Abortion Clinic

You're a murderer.
And you were late!

She gavel-slams facts to the point
like the two pink lines that showed up earlier.
My nose recounts the scented tampons abandoned
at the bottom of my bathroom drawer.
They were all I could smell after my dinner
floated in a toilet bowl of life-changing
piss. Bubble yellow brilliant as dirty ocean grief.
Haunted by want, desires that had to die:
dreams of marriage, my holy career, a second
bedroom that could have been a nursery
with wallpaper the shade of *Your daddy said*
he loved me once [but told his wife forever].

Amy's a mom of six, about to be seven.
She's made of a lamb's spool that I'm not.
She married her high school sweetheart, Jesse,
on the premise of procreation, picture-perfect piety.
Her favorite title: handmaiden.
I try to tell her the cold gel force was suicide,
not murder. I'm killing myself in God's image.
Judge Amy shakes her South Bend head,
grips the steering wheel, and prepares a sermon.

My eyes squirm ahead, trying to avoid reading the bumper sticker
on the bright red F-150 pickup truck in front of Amy's minivan.
An obnoxious baby made of red, white, and blue
hugs a ribbon that reads:
DEFEND THE DEFENSELESS

The decal shatters me more than any car wreck or soldier ever did.
Amy is happy Planned Parenthood had me look at the heartbeat.
It's law here in the South.
Amy wishes more states did that.
She's sure she can make that happen.
All you murderers should hear that sound for the rest of your lives.

I'd record it if I could.
Play it on repeat,
outside your windows
when you're asleep.
Set it as your alarm.
On repeat,
I want you to wake up to the sound of that
heartbeat.
Murderer.

I want to tell her that my mother calls me daughter,
my brother calls me sister,
and there's a man her Jesus forgave
who once called me lover
and I believed I was worthy.

But none of those things matter.
She's giving me my life sentence.
I am ready to hear it.
I agree with the enormity and its conditions.
I know what I am.
I know what I am without.

Bless my heart, I'm a murderer
and she's a cunt.
And I'm thankful I'm not driving home alone.

Oil Changed

I daydream about getting an oil change without
pretending to have a boyfriend or standing up straight
enough to not hunch my back when I get the Ladies' Day
special on a Tuesday afternoon instead of grabbing lunch.

The mechanic thinks I don't know anything
about fixing things stronger than myself.
He's right. I have a few exes that would agree.
Like stray pups, I, their bitch, nursed them back to healthier egos.

Their floppy ears and swollen heads could not fit in homes
we rented and missed payments on.
I couldn't afford any of them and the space they took up in my skirt,
my medical bills, my body.

So I drove miles away in a car I leased and missed payments on.
I would order shots and stay up late on borrowed time
and credit card fees, racking up points to travel somewhere
my trauma could never afford to live.

Pressing ignore to 1-800 numbers with my back flat
against the linoleum when someone in the next stall
leans over to listen to my overpour of hunger.
How tough on my stomach to disappoint myself for a reaction.

Maxing out on flashy growth is expensive
when I never knew the cost of being alone.
I looked for love in the form of men I could text
from the oil change place, or the nail salon, or the therapist's couch.

Others didn't have to know the details of my bedroom.
None of the hopeful imaginary in my head ever landed
a home in a place where oil spilled.

Mothers & Daughters

Shame hangs like misguided anchors
because we beg for the same rite of relation.
We yearn for someone to hold us rocksteady
like a lighthouse during a storm,
someone to batter and wash our veins,
hurt us or harm us, like a toothache,
cake icing, or a dog
being run over, dragged down,
a favorite girlfriend
cheating on you with the
class bully. I can make this list
as fucked up as I need to or —
the kind nurse's arms
you plunge into when
your war hero father dies over
the bathroom toilet.
The shared link with
the only other woman
in the world who could
appreciate this handed-down
runoff of hope.

I Pencil Grieving You in My Planner

1	2	3
Attend that guy's party. Order three new bras that boost my confidence. Give myself enough support to look like my dad isn't dying.	Apply to some big-girl job, determined to make money and leave this town behind. Pay the bills handed to me as a birthright for being born in a single-parent household. Buy waterproof mascara.	Refinance my face and enroll in a class to learn to smile more. Stop answering my phone. It's always bad news or loan collectors. Not sure what scares me more these days. Death or my growing interest in it.
6 MRSA. Wear a hazmat suit to see his sweaty body. Attend that guy's first and only art exhibit — hanging from these twinkly lights — piss-yellow bags float in front of my eyes in the city I escape to. Buy new shoes on Amazon because magic carpets are out of stock.	**7** Start applying for jobs. Out of state. Look up plane tickets. Print an itinerary of how to cope from far away. Make myself smaller.	**8** RIP everything up by midnight. Skip breakfast. Skip lunch. Skip dinner.
11 Hospital. Another art exhibit. My turn.		

4 Attend an open bar from 3pm – 6pm. Dinner. Taco Bell with that guy. Hospital. Uber home.	5 Skip work or maybe it's closed. I don't know anymore. Call hospice. Pretend I dial the wrong number when they ask for his name.	
9 Drink so badly that my phone won't wake up so that I can finally ask for *help* when I think I should.	10 Attend that guy's burial at 10am. Order a new planner. Learn to grieve without reminders.	

Three Icebreakers by Someone with Dead Daddy Issues

Part 1. Three Lies and a Truth

1. He was always present on my worst of days.
2. We share a name.
3. He's so much bigger in death than in life.
4. I could have called him father.

Part 2. Twenty-One Questions: A Game of Yes or No

Is a child's blood fifty percent of their father's?
If I die from addiction is it considered natural because it came from my dad?
Did my dad's casket rest in exhausted wet earth with no threat of relapse?
Did my boozebrain thank those who braved dirty Jersey to pay respects?
Was I fluent enough to cry in the language the priest prayed in?
Did my fatherless tongue lap at brown-bagged pain?
Has Father's Day gotten easier without the threat of his belligerence?
Can I find his ghost on the table of diners, atop the dark pee-bag mustard disco fries?
Can I feel his corner store spirit in cold coffee cups in church basements?
Have ten summers come and winters stay as lonely as mourning in February?
Did my father lose the battle the year I became legal enough to purchase his poison?
Did I spend all of my twenty-first birthday attempting to be God?
Would my father attend the saddrunk party if he could?
Would he recognize me if he saw me aged and a sober mother?
Is the last time Pops saw me at my eighth grade prom?
Was he drunk on how my beggar's body clung to thrift craftsmanship?
Is that why he called me a bitch and covered his eyes?
Would he call me a bitch now or would he call me his girl?
Would he forgive me for not seeing him at the end?
Can I forgive myself?
Is pain hereditary?

Part 3: The Finale: Would You Rather?

Have my nine-pound, jaundice-ridden body swaddled with my
daddy's lullaby in '88?
Have my father's cracked hands hold my bachelor's degree in '08?

Have my dad sit front-row at my graduation, half beaming like a
broken marquee?
Have a Sweet Caroline sing-along where we and our ghosts are
all hands entwined, drunk and happy, in the East Village?

Let me drive drunk over a bridge and its troubled waters to find
a partner?
Let me sleep drunk over and over with untrustworthy men with
the scent of your past?

Sit with me during his final days and remind me I can hold it together?
Lay with me during those first days and remind me I
need nourishment, too?

Erase his criminal record and rewrite his narrative as father of the
bride and dad of the year?
Erase the darkness I carry and publish my truth as daughter and
mother of letting go?

The Four Stages of Death: Ode to Louie

Within four minutes of death,
the human body starts decomposing.
Similar to grief, death happens in stages.
My grief is a death.

IV.

Makeup for the dead starts at $250 for one handsome goodbye.
It is more expensive to de-purple bruising at your funeral
than at your wedding.
I wonder if the windshield fragments sparkled in your brown face
and if they held glint while hard to remove.

You were dressed in a Patrick Ewing jersey
and a fitted Yankees cap to hold in your brain.
The paint on your face was patchier than my faded Martens.
You laid still. Somebody's mama started crying.

We left you to fade into alabaster after paying our respects.
Skeletonization is the fourth and final stage.
Bones
still trying to hold on.

III.

Within a week, decay sets in and bargaining begins
between what will become liquid and what will become dust.
Joy leaks
out of hair and teeth.

Depending on trauma and temperature,
a body weeps itself into water.
Speed snarls at decisions,
a funeral must take place before the body becomes a burden.

II.

Within twenty-four to seventy-two hours,
anger sets in,
and the corpse
will double in size.

Blood cells burst fierce from broken vessels,
bloating turns body to buffet,
insects begin to feast with fury.
You were my first open casket.

I was twelve. You are always fifteen.

You and my brother,
ghost stop signs in time,
two Hispanic men,
dead from various violent vices.

I was twelve, a nerd,
never allowed on the streets,
you were a teenager hardened by gangs,
dead a week before eighth-grade graduation.

You died stealing a car and I robbed your story to write a poem.
Unable to tell one funeral from another,
I never mentioned my brother in the lines on survival.
He remained an unused cameo, some other poet's rite to mourn.

I.

The first stage is autolysis, self-digestion.
I'm not sure what stage I'm in yet,
but I write this down to remember you, Louie. A second attempt in verse
because that's how I grieve.

Chance Encounter [with Redemption & a bus ticket]

I once shared a cab with Charlie Sheen and he didn't make a move
other than tipping
over like someone's bottled uncle and telling me I was pretty and asking
if I had cocaine and I didn't, so we listened to Bob Marley serene as a sage
breeze wailing to us about Redemption as the driver became something
private and escort, high on navigating through the buses
and the bodies, the dead, and the pedestrians of New York.

We rode uncharted, undisguised, tires slicked with Times Square,
but quiet for a moment of soberness when the thunder of our lives
hummed to a halt *(none but ourselves freeing our minds)*
or I imagine that's when the rain gathered up and
when lightning burned down a bodega in Spanish Harlem.
Where were we going, Carlos?

Did you see that? a whisper.
I did, but I can't, a tiger whose blood became a dream.

What were we doing? Elbow-pressed vessels in drunk echoes together
and our need to be needed and our lessons being forgotten,
like rent, bills, and wedding bands. Two junkies with so much junk.
Manhattan felt like a place for chance encounters addictive enough
to take lines for,
almost willing to compose a book —

until I saw the shadows of someone who looked celebrity
and looked mirrored madman monster
and looked at me
and I caught a bus home alone,
too poor for pirates to rob my pretty.

In Four Minutes This Peestick Makes Me Mom

after Jonathan Safran Foer

What's my favorite version of my name? Is the name I wear best the one
I have owned for the shortest amount of time? Is it the one laboring its
cents into my paycheck? Or the one written on the card my gynecologist
sent me? Have I been reduced to a fake holiday, Hallmark bear, and the
guilt of men around the world once a year? Is every man's weakness his
mother? Do I dance in twilight with crust nestled asleep in my eyes?
My body recites its mistakes: does that make me sad or exhausted?
Which feels worse: going days hungry for sex? Or going days hungry
for apologies? Is being fucked the same kinda despair if you don't have
a choice? Have I googled if the world has more guns than children?
Have I lost friends I never had? Am I aware of what is created when
my adulthood failures kiss my childhood hopes at 3 am? Can I recall
what sunrise after pushing under a cloth mask in a pandemic looks like?
Stretch-marked, scary, breathless, splendid? If I cherish the smallest
milestones, can I count the crinkles in my daughter's eyes? If an angel
exists, is it because I birthed her? Are pages another form of limbs? Word
count, limb count, does the body hear I love you even when there are no
sounds? What is it about giving myself to another that is so heartbreaking,
obvious, and beautiful? Why does it give me purpose? How do I feel?
What is my favorite name? Is my name Mother? Or is it Poet?

Wash the Dishes

I wash the dishes, cake my nails in oil and grime
from some stew or chili I made when I was too
angry or sad to have a conversation.
Sometimes I cook or clean or do something
with my hands to channel why I feel the way I do
or why I don't feel the way you do.
Anxiety has a way of making you feel useless
or productive or sometimes uselessly productive.

I mean to say, sometimes I wash the dishes
so that I can wash the thoughts away,
wash the worry,
wash the doom, dead, and dread,
wash the filth of what-ifs,
submerge the bowl of my depressants.
Sometimes I scream into bubbles of dirt
hoping to see a cleaner reflection
at the bottom of the sink.

I shout into the dirty so that the dishes,
the laundry, the thoughts
can be somewhere cleaner, unsoiled.
A pancaked prayer in a downstairs kitchen basin,
chores me into something.
Slow, spic and span,
catch speed.

Dawn.
Bubbles.
Sponge.
Plates.
Wash the dishes.
I become a grocery/chore list.
Honey, do me.

Margarita

after Patricia Smith

Margarita is who my mother wanted me to be.
Flaquita in flowery tang presence
somewhere outside the Garden State Parkway
or inside a forget-me-not pinata,
eighty-cent plastic booze bottle Borinquen baby
blossoming and spilling at my mama's hooded eyes.
If I was Margarita,
Big Margaret, my mom, would be
lucky and not twice Puerto Rican
divorced, and I would sprout more
beautiful Boricua princesas.
They'd be fluent in charm.
Heritage rich on native tongue.
Some brown. Some pink. Trigueña.
Margarita. Damn.
I imagine I could have a
whole casita of Margaritas.
But my mom wasn't lucky.
I didn't become anything more than
someone that played bad with tequila.
Someone who needs a mixer of a man
to taste mas fresca.
Margarita, a tart limona grown
from vines around the world.
Making sure to ride the surprise sweetness
of sour before bad news knocks her down.
Margarita, she'd have it all together,
or at minimum, be able to outdrink the negative of a day.

TEN STEPS TO STOP YOURSELF FROM DROWNING (A POET'S EDITION)

The truth is that most drownings are preventable, but you must understand the facts and know how to prevent it from happening.
— excerpt from StopDrowningNow's Drowning Statistics Keynote

1. Don't read sad poetry — words will meld and grab the reach of your bones, of your metaphor. It's the booze of the Bard. It will weigh you down.

2. Swear to be good and pretend you're God. Walk on water and make believers out of your begotten.

3. Don't fall in love with devices of fuck-me-over plastic. Cheap canoes will crack. The only thing that will save you already exists within you.

4. Leave voicemails even if someone might not listen. Write letters. Mail care packages and hold no resentment. Do something to surprise someone because butterflies in stomachs can be life jackets for friends lost to the waves.

5. Make sure to save yourself before trying to save someone else. Words mean nothing if there's no one to hear them.

6. Learn to swim even when you are drenched and dampened from the day. Learn CPR. Continue Poetry Regardless.

7. You think this shit can kill you? It will.

8. Build up fences around anything that may cause you to think less of your surroundings.

9. Make so much noise it fills your lungs and threatens to shoot geysers of grief. There is nothing silent about how you will leave this Earth.

10. Don't go at this alone. Look for a life/guard.

June is Here

He's dead. Jun is dead.

Moments before felt foreign and far, a smeared postcard of sound.
There was a ring. My eyes devoured images of ordinary kids
getting into ordinary trouble with a laugh track for the highs.
Then a wail. The howl of her cries signaled new lows.

Then a thump. Too frightened to go towards the source
of the grievous noise, my young legs rooted in safety, I dared
myself to move. Inching closer toward bravery that otherwise
never would have existed, I aged ten years in ten seconds.

She was spread, broken, and bawling. A wild mother
bird that realized her nest was now in ruins. I held
her close, begging her tears to piece her wings
back together so that we pilot away from pain.

It had been two weeks since we last had a call
from my brother. Far from home, he would always call
when he was on a long drive or a certain song

came on. His idea of comfort started with a ring
and ended with an *I love you*. My mom never admitted favorites
but sat by the phone each night in Sunday's best with a toothy grin.

He taught me how to swim and ride a bike, promising
we'd explore worlds with our muscles and pedals as pillars.
Not only her first son, he was the captain of my adventures.

Until two men thought he looked better
beaten on the side of the road than in any photo
at my wedding.

It would be four days before they found his body.
It would be two years of trials before a sentence.
It would be ten years of medicine to get my mom to sleep.
It would be a lifetime of waiting for his voice to come
through the other line.

It is a Saturday when I call her, some twenty years later.
There is a ring. She answers out of breath.
She now waits until the last minute to pick up,
bad news no longer gets priority.

Hey Mom.
There is a small wail. I hear her draw a deep breath,
unseen armor her aged body has refined and trusted.
She's here. June is here.

Then a tiny thump. The babe beats
a wrinkled fist against the receiver. My mother weeps
into the phone and I clutch it and my baby as close as I can,
unable to end the call until we say *I love you.*

Crier's Apparatus

My heaving chest dares to say clean me
like mashed potato postpartum
mother in the slow-to-rise aisle.
The moist ache of my life goes *slosh, slosh, slosh.*
My days are speechless sobs in bodegas
and mid-traffic breakdowns.
How alive and dead this world can be all at once.
Often, technology assists with flooding my face—
for friend requests from rapists,
for weeping when I see memories
of my dead brother on Facebook.
His birthday landed on last week's school shooting.
Do I mark my baby safe before I remember *Happy Birthday?*
Panic plants saltwater begonias in the pit
of my stomach's yearning familial bite.
I sometimes grow a smile that collapses
my face like a water lily from all her innocent joy.
The machine in me never knows if the world cares more
for my family's safety or for organ chunks of pain at a time.
Nonetheless, I scoop my daughter up from the haven of daycare.
I whistle a bulletproof birthday candle out in the May wind.
My baby runs two small feet, *pit, pat, pat,*
to me, a star-wide grin delirious to see my love.
How devastating to feel such rich blue emotion.
Pools from the riverbeds of my eyes skate
to the hope of her periwinkle smile.
I become a sprinkler at home, the place where we are safest.
This haven where you cannot separate
woman from faucet.

Love an Abecedarian

All the poems I write have a piece of you in them.
But, this one here is my way of saying — *hi.*
Call this one yours.
Dearest love —

everyone's been writing
for thousands of years.
Gorgeous words that can
honor or humiliate someone.

I wrote this one for you,
just for you.
Know this — it's
Love. And it's *you.* And

Me.
Not just in the poems that are shared between us.
Often. Or in the lyrics of snores on pillows. But in the way my
pen knows of no other siren song.

Quiet, like an earth shake.
Rumbling at its drum core,
so badly wanting
to

undress you.
Veins and quatrains on display, a
way with words when you first said you're my
biggest fan. A stranger solving for
X of the mess and beauty within me.

You, the thesis in every melody from *A* to
Z.

At the Altar of My Minutiae

My mother places red, white, and blue bruised
second-hand rosary beads next to fish, bread, this

mother matronsaint body of mine— all small in the same room.
She tsks in a positive way, one

which Southern well-mannered belle mothers can produce
who believe in hell and

something higher, gentler, better
at controlling everything. Part of the plan.

I am closer to becoming
happy. Resplendent.

She means thinner, but says happy.
I'm the only one that has figured this out.

My mother, poster parent of wanting pageants with her break-
fast, me in ribbons, loves when my hair

is straighter, longer, leaner, hangs loose
around my petite toy torso. The way to be seen

is the act of being unseen when all but the Devil bails,
and you exist, kinda like God. Her Southern drawl pours over

biscuits, gravy, and taffies and tales of how to get into heaven.
I stand, tattered, tatted, Barbie of beatings

and belongings, listening heartears wide, as best I can,
not sharing stories that are not my own.

I study her measured meter for meeting joy
I have been hurt to train under this god.

I think disciple.
I bleed gospel.

She drabs on until she mentions the belly fat
of my child's giggle, and I ask her

if all these deaths were part of the plan?
She doesn't stop her sermon, *Of course, Sabrina,*

moves on to how adorable my daughter is,
how prodigy, how malleable.

Maybe it was the way in which the bruised
indigo ego of my identity crisis collapsed my

reflection in the mirror that morning or the way my ex-
boss sent me a mess-

age and my back stood tangled in a sash in the Texas Hill Country,
across the room from the confidence of the Colorado River.

Tons of petite particulars — surely part of the plan.
I pause — remember the Gospel of John and reports

that Jesus' bony son used five loaves to feed five thousand,
I pause again — ask my mother, why am I starving?

My Friend's Husband Verbally Abuses Her and I Say Nothing Because I Am Afraid To(o)

My dad hit my mom once.
It's not fully my story to tell —
except I will say my father loved my mother.
He also had his demons.
And sometimes, despite the dedication, the demons win.
I've been guilty of that.
And it was that hit that would then become my origin story —
how my mother, dressed in battered dignity
supported by my uncle, wild with the strongest growl,
chose to leave at that moment.
Raise her kids. Raise them well and
raise them kind. Raise them with hope.
Didn't speak any of my daddy except to say
he was rotten once, but still as green and whole as a
granny apple when she first saw him dangling like a kid
perched above a tree smiling her strawberry way.
I grew up lost in a lineage's maze puzzle, not fitting anywhere.
It isn't until I'm in the car with my best friend and her husband.
She gives him a direction; he calls her stupid without calling her stupid.
Says she is directionless, without following the directions. He says this
is why women shouldn't drive. Me. In the backseat, with my DUI
past and my crippling driving anxiety now, stares at the cows grazing
on the side of the southern highway road.
Y'all see those huge brown cows?
Not daring to be the one in that moment to turn history and
separate child from father,
create other lost puzzles with lasting scenes and scars on repeat.

The Dentist

He holds my sober-for-this-appointment brain in his sterile hands.
Mister Machismo with kind blue letterman eyes.

All his nurses practice their smiles, straighten backs of teeth, pucker,
flirt when he walks by. My hysterical sobs slice

his gendered bullshit. I have a knack
for turning frat parties into funerals.

He pretends to see something precious in my tremble —
my high deductible or pity from my waiting room panic attack.

He asks what's the one thing that makes a young woman with long legs
crouch like a meek lamb west of Slaughter's Lane?

I struggle more with his presumptive ask of only *one* thing than his stare
down my shirt. How do I say my ex-lover with similar eyes to the dentist,

took and caused an entire galaxy of pain and caused me to
neglect simple oral hygiene and humane affirmation?

How, every day, I find it hard to brush off that women like me
are being told our sacrificed parts are our ugliest?

How, contrary to all of this, I stay clean and beautiful because
I cry the hardest in the shower where I see my robbed nakedness?

How do I say, *hi, my name spells out a trigger warning?*
Landing on deaf ears, Dr. Echo implores further and

something moves under my rib cage, nostrils splayed,
teeth shaking in their rotten abandoned sockets and I say:

The sound. I hear it all too close for comfort.
and what I meant to say is:

I can hear burnt rubber tracks, tabs left unpaid,
lowered caskets, heartbeats stop and speed on monitors.

I'm in a car suspended —Frogger turned near-dead-drunk ballerina,
and the sound of my mother's moans scare ants to denture deathbeds.

He must see it then — a flash in my pregnant mouth of decay and secrets.
He asks if he could hold my ears and scalpel it to silence.

I cry uglier and whisperweep, *please.*
I cling to his latexed sincerity and beg

to be healed and wake from life-destroying
cavities I keep creating for myself.

On Becoming Vegetable

Bacon is out of stock again during the pandemic.
Dismissed and unable to move,
I am reduced to making chili for dinner.

My husband is pleased with me.
He is always pleased with me.
Who knew being 693 days alone together

could make someone fall
even more in love?
But hey, that could be another poem.

The point here is the chili.
It is a recipe I hold close
which is to mean I Google enough chilis

that I have my favorite.
Bookmark my heart in a digital landscape.
I skim down to the lines that make it fulfilling,

Dolloped in sour, I bathe myself in broth
after a hard day of drab,
looking for sustenance,
and knowing — all I have left is me.

Like a guilty russet potato
in some chili
out of place.

No, I am not *even*
a fucking vegetable.
Vegetarian myself apart.

I am something
without root,
without meat.

The Fire or the Kindling

My loyal mate dips his soft nuzzles down
to my navel. Outside, desperate; fog, USA dumpfire;
my heart, an excavation site full of ashes of us
splayed against satin and eight hundred thread count.
The sunk of me, threadbare —
feeling old earth, molten lava.
This mama — knowing men seek to
trap-shackle these limbs until I collapse.
My dear beau wants to know what motivates
me to stay here if not for the hellfire temptation
of resistance I have come to strike/match myself.
Trauma and heartache can hold peace in a poem.
I write as often as I rage these days.
Quiet. Fan the flames.
I have always known my vulnerability is what
would allow me to build bridges with *brujas,*
little did I know being woman in this land meant only
becoming a breeder's boarding house ablaze.
My sweet husband, doused in Jack's honey bourbon, holds my hips
and begs me to tell him what causes the ruby roof of me to come
tumbling into debris?
Kindling. It's the kindling,
all but violence, I hear the small of our daughter wail in her crib
midafternoon nap zapped, dreams of dragons, freedom, of magic,
It's kindling.

I Stand Up for Myself and My Husband Calls It Sabotage

To be wife is to be lips steel, gaping, tight,
open like a mouth, like the wedding band
around his finger, or a rifle's trigger.
Wife gives body like goldfinches give
their sugary clementine song to the
morning sky.

He doesn't wake up to see any pretty Texas
Hill sunrise. He snores ungrateful and loud. He pisses and
farts himself awake. Doesn't say good morning
until his coffee makes him kind and lucid.
I don't sleep anymore, but my hands leap to
his offer of morning coffee.
Iced, please.

I wife too constant like stark naked winds before
a textbook hurricane slams down for the night.
I recognize that to be a wife is to plant a fruitful
garden. A garden that does not wilt with the cruel moss
my poems reveal about their makers. Legs wide apart,
I yell sometimes — *see and sniff me!*
I thrust into visibility as he coils.
My husband, defensive, beer-bellied past swung open,
winces. I win. He rages, calling it sabotage.
My husband thinks he's always right.

NOT TODAY / DEATH

the mangled dead rabbit / no longer has its dusk blue bunny eyes /
I am not sure how they popped forward and piled cardinal red /
in the scorching gravel driveway / I refuse to teach about the dead /

summoning musty cardboard / hurried mindful pulling death down /
Every move matters and conversation must flow
on to prevent a pause that can ruin a family's innocent glow /

my babe / barely bird, barely girl / chirps in car, full of song /
I become intent hawk / destined to outlive prey falling from sky tomb /
I feed life / not today / death / my eyes inspect / covet / consume

Frailty

Within thirty-something years of life, I thought old people
were frail bags of bones dragging at snail speed because
they no longer could go fast like lightning.
No drive, no direction, broken down cars without engines.
Depleted wrought machines lost in time, I scoff at their clocks.
How weak!
In the frost of one winter, though, I came to realize they have been
practicing the joy of making their hourglasses slow down.
Holding the sunshine before admiring the sunset.
Having conversations before deploying metal.
How weak I was to think the wiser would be willing
their bodies to do anything other than crave eternal.

Reverse Aisle Walk Down the Entryway of Our New Home

I.

Splintered fruit fell to the floor in the hollow home.
Spread streaks of rouge violet into the baseboards of romance.
Snaked up creating an ivy distance that plumps open a floor plan.
Heavy becomes an intimate blanket, down in discomfort.
Piles of love letters on napkins long forgotten,
all folding and collapsing into cracked concrete parts.
All a reminder —
everything can become past due if you ignore it enough.

II.

Nature has no expiration, but humans do.
Full bellies swoosh in dry, dead air where we allow
and because our bodies no longer wear gold rings that orbit,
he and I have learned to whisperwaltz around all twelve rooms.
An alcoholic's concerto playing the lowest notes,
Van Morrison crackling through his bourbon.
Once the kitchen brimmed with love and a
mantle of wedding photos, now a stifling oven.

In the moonlight eve, I bathe myself like a violent wave of
an ocean orange sunset.
The steamy red hut of my arms covers my boobs in a flash
as once-stargazer averts his eyes.
He is a familiar hazy sky of matches with no strike.
Sorry, I didn't realize you were here.
I ache for land and ground and sun
thunder in (re)verse my ash cherry ballerina lips
croak, '*I'm sorry, too.*'

III.

Sometimes *I'm sorry* means *I love you.*
Sometimes the record ends without ever making a sound.

I Scramble to Recite bell hooks When My Daughter Asks Me About Our Dead Family

Children can be curious green kites
untethered with words and language
landscapes at tip-of-tongue, balloon buoyancy
floating in questions about what goes missing.
The forgotten toy in the dark classroom.
The uncle she never met in the picture.
The father she never met in the picture.
The baby in her mama's mind's bathroom.
They expect adults to walk like sturdy skyscrapers
after they dance on elder graves,
place pictures on the mantle, and write
handsome poems to the drunken dead.
And because I cannot tell my daughter I might die, too,
I tell her bell hooks says we only learn to lie
because we are too hungry and too lonely
to hurt those who love us.
She isn't three yet and doesn't speak English
very well, my daughter blinks back,
Bell book, mama?
But her mama is a poet so I laugh and place
my grubgrey ink-stained paws next to hers and
speak to soothe the hurt that hangs above my fireplace.
Today, I choose to meditate on love.
I tell her there is melted ice cream living in the dirty
chest of my heart. There is a tooth so loose
I keep swallowing my youth when she begs for answers.
There is a bookshelf with unreturned books in a library
called every person your mommy loves dies and yes, that's the truth,
But lucky for her, the library is closed because the last book
on how to live an extraordinary life is too busy falling in love
with her and her big questions and etching it all down,
like a family tree uplifted in bloom for the first time.

Flowers Would Bloom

Sometimes I think if Jesus freed his hands, he'd wipe nails away
and bounties of flowers would bloom in the holes.

The ghost of survival would wait for the opportune moment
to spread steady vibrant joy in a place of robbed dreams.

I like to think if forgiveness was planted at gravesites,
begonias would be more popular than dogs.

Imagine the world running wild with ranunculus and lavender
pawing at our heels and not gun violence

dropping us to our knees.
Imagine how sublime it'd be to see a sky of rainbow daffodils

and not hide behind a desk during an active shooter drill.
Imagine young children practicing writing script and poetry,

not perfecting how to mark themselves safe on social media.
I'm safe, a metaphor for today. I thought I would die and didn't.

Sometimes I think if Jesus freed his hands,
he'd pray for flowers like lilies or marigolds.

Sometimes I think we're only God in our final edits.
Sometimes I feel like I'm the bruised seed.

Whisper Street

Down by the Hudson River hotdog stand on Bowery, where
$3 pashmina
is bartered beside checks cashing into fresh Nikes, Katz's Deli,
fried chicken,
and devil's lettuce, the littered concert stubs stapled me into a woman.

On the college reverie streets of New York City, I found the bravado
in my courage
by witnessing everyday poets and angels on subway rides at Penn
Station at 2 am,
under an umbrella near the sketchy adult store comedy club on East 2nd.

New York City, a concrete ocean of chance encounters and
minimum waged humility,
Rockefeller grit to be able to find myself every day in the metallic glean
of a morning after A train.

I transformed into a pickup truck spilling my daddy issues and
hurling myself into a crowded highway
of first jobs, hand jobs, drinks, and lines on the table, the
black-tinted cabs near the 1

train that said: *free ride for pretty girls like you.*

I'd like to take a ride downtown to the George Washington Bridge.
I'd like to drown, sir. Can you fix me?

Dizzy, only after I tend to the garden of my evergreen thoughts,
New York City, a smog oasis, gases itself into my brain.

I see you. Go home, you've relapsed, Lady Liberty.
There are no torches, no Bibles, no lips to seek or mascara or Merlot.

There are only hollering bridges of traffic and people reunited near places
where people reunited and departed for hundreds of years and
will continue. Repeat.

The plane at JFK departs and I've never heard a more
heartbreaking rageful hum above.
Can a promise break the sound barrier?

No matter how many times I've edited New York City out of my life's manuscript,
she keeps showing up when I wail myself awake on Whisper Street.

Artbreak

Divorce strikes against raw off-white
walls at the close of a firecracker June.
The word trickles down, with
new home keys lunged forward
with Latina might, and I take a stand.
My husband, two minutes ago masterpiece,
now stranger, who is sorry, weepy, and slumping.
Tragedies look artful
to anyone on the outside.
Museum soul window open, tears waterfall,
I must look like a suburban pietà.
Do not pray or beg me like a god
who grants forgiveness and mercy
over a dead lying body.
I am not Jesus, not his mother, and
I often wear grudges like scarves
I wish to strangle across pale alcoholic necks.
Under yesterday's shadow,
I swallowed two pills whole,
and willed hell to exist for him.
I am human and cracked porcelain
and sublime and there is no completeness
I've held on to since I've left the womb.
No need for a reminder that
I am someone's mother.
I know what is profound and what is pathetic.
I know art from criminal and I'm not going
anywhere, only breaking everywhere.

I Have to Accept That All of It Will Not Last

In spring sangria's sunrise and hues arise,
in the quiver of my lover's caress,
beneath brown, oversized, and wise Ray-Bans,
in the haze of too many vodka sodas
and big fat fingers that text in excess,
in the closet kissing where irony resides,
in the nightmare and visitor in my lover's head,
in the shaggy-haired lead singer's orbs
screambleeding his heart toward mine,
in the mmph of live poetry readings,
in sink piled high with pesto-laden problems,
in my pandemic pregnancy and a labored mask,
in anguish after my absent father dies,
in the flutter of a boy scout's proposal,
in the empty uptown, downtown apartment,
in the candlelight of my baby's first birthday wish,
in the honesty of the first sober email,
in the drunk of a scrawled letter and how it enthralls,
in the summer, winter —
fall. I must accept that all of it will not last.

ACKNOWLEDGMENTS

My heartfelt gratitude to the following publications in which earlier versions of these poems first had a home:

All My Relations, The Bitchin' Kitsch: "June is Here"

Ample Remains: "Hormones and Clapton During First Period"

Anti-Heroin Chic: "In Two Minutes This Test Calls Me Mom" now titled "In Four Minutes This Peestick Makes Me Mom"

Birmingham Arts Journal: "Flowers Would Bloom"

Exposition Review: "I Pencil Grieving You Into My Planner"

Gnashing Teeth Publishing: "The Day I Grew Boobs" now titled "Ode to the Day I Grew Boobs"

Gulf Stream Magazine: "OK, I'm Finally Ready to Admit My Faults" now titled "Admission of My Most Expensive Fault"

Olney Magazine: "Three Icebreakers by Someone with Dead Daddy Issues"

Sledgehammer Lit: "Ten Steps to Stop Yourself from Drowning (A Poet's Edition)"

West Trade Review: "alternate names for damaged women" now titled "Otro Nombre"

Wrongdoing Magazine: "An Ode to An Alternate Universe In Which Amy Coney Barrett Drives Me to the Abortion Clinic" now titled "Ode to Amy Coney Barret Driving Me to the Abortion Clinic"

A BIT OF THANKS —

There is no me without others. Thank you to the higher power that allows my stories to live surrounded by company.

My mother is present in all my stories because she is present in every way I react to a situation, where I can find hope, the process I use to cope with joy, and the processes I have formed to deal with other emotions. Thank you for showing me that an education is the most valuable thing and stressing happiness over career. Honesty over cover. Kindness over wealth. Vulnerability over pride. You have made me better every day.

For my father (who is no longer with us), thank you for instilling in me the stubbornness and rage. The grit. The hustle. The spice. The sazón. You exist in every step I take with the swagger and confidence I have learned to own and sow. You owned your skin and when you shone, there was nothing brighter. I am sorry for not showing mercy sooner. I hope to get another chance. I hope it's right now.

For my siblings — Jun, Eddie, Chris, Laura — you mean so much to me. I hope there is something in here that can give you hope, too. I love you. Thank you for having my back through the life I lived behind these stories.

For my sweetest baby poet, K, oh, baby, thank you. I love you more than I can write or voice note and that's a LOT. Thank you for teaching me that being present is all we have. Brave truth is the only direction.

For my bonus parents, John and Ginnie, thank you for allowing me time in your family and sharing your music and spirit.

For my extended *familia*, both by blood, marriage, and not, all ten uncles and seven aunts and three hundred cousins, forty-seven little second cousins; y'all are all so loud and weird and I can't do life without you. Thank you for existing with me, and being your authentic selves in such a way I grew to be comfortable in my skin. You're about half my readership. You exist in every lyric and on every playlist. Let's dance with and for one another. Side by side. *Para siempre.*

To Titi Pinkie, thank you for always seeing me in a brave way. You mean everything to me and have turned my biggest breakdowns into sheer laughter and love and presence. You, my *tia*, are a testament to queen. You are a diamond. *Te amo.*

For my closer-than-fam besties and their generous, loving families — pre-pandemic and before I had boobs — Megan, Pamela, Syreeta, Carlos, Kelly, Yury, Hawwa, Chrissy, Jen, Jose, Jon, Mark — thank you for safety when I felt I did not have any. You kept me alive with love, laughter, and hope when I wasn't sure about the good in the world anymore.

To my local fam that have kept me afloat in numerous ways through trips, walks, facetime, and hugs — Vanessa, Amy, Sam, Steve, Janelle, Joe, Robin, Kari, Stela, Hana, Celeste, Ashleigh, Courtney, Tyree, Cortney, Kayte, Ayanna, Joey, Pete, Alec, Lizzie, Chris B., Ben, Ashten, Taylor, Kathleen D., Jack, Greer, Ash, Nisha, Peggy, Khalim, Kat, Sinead, Jacob, Sarah, Matt, Gracie, Jasmin, Christian, and the coffee roasters at the Buda Market.

For my writing besties — y'all could take up a whole ass book, too, but here I go: Dennis Hinrichsen, Miyagi, thank you for sharing your brilliance and keeping me in the group. Melissa Sussens, you are kind, fierce, and intelligent. Thank you for always making me want to do better always. Jo, my goodness, Jo, your heart and words are the definition of poetry. Thank you. Masaki, you saw me before I saw myself. Thank you for continuing to be that real energy I need. Native Child Brown, you welcomed me with mama-arms and saw me, oh how I see the moon in your timeless goddess presence. Thank you, queen. Sheleen McElhinney, thank you for telling me this was possible and showing me the way. You have no idea how much I admire you. I love you. Adam Montri, for cultivating friendship where we all needed it most and providing warmth. Diane Lato, sister, thank you.

I could go on and on but more so thanks to the following writers: Katie Mueller, Sita Gaia, Danielle Low Waters, Kyrsta Morehouse, Erica Abbott, Valerie Nies, Carson Wolfe, Miriam Kramer, Beck Anson, Kika Man, Jason Terry, James Roach, Nikki Allen, Rocio Franco, Carlos Andrés Gómez, Karla Cordero, Ben Weakley, Desiare, Judith O, Kym Mac, Caroline Earleywine, and Andie Jones.

To my teachers and mentors along the way — I could hug you until my heart stops beating. Thank you for giving me a space to share and grow. You cultivated not only community in your spaces, but you cultivated compassion as craft, and precision as a bonus element — Karen Haynes, Camille Earle, Neel Khichi, Matthew Gironda, Brendan Rippey, Jessica Flores, Stephanie Aiyeku, Frances Wilson, Megan Falley, Andrea Gibson, Buddy Wakefield, Jon Sands, Phil Kaye, Desiree Delgiacommo, Chondra

& Claudio Sanchez, COTF, Seema Reza and the entire Community Building Arts community.

To classmates in Emotional Historians and Poems That Don't Suck, I never knew my heart could grow bigger via Zoom. Y'all are some sorcerers of light and poems. Courtney LeBlanc, how have you uplifted me through this? How? While doing your own life? I will forever be grateful. Thank you for all the notes. I will write until my arms bleed. I promise.

For my therapists, Tamar, Mylah, and Juana, y'all really let me talk through the rough draft version of these poems. Thanks for watering my growth and saving me from drowning. For listening. For advocating. For praising me when no one did.

To my publisher and DERRICK BROWN — holy thank you. Thank you for breathing life into these pages. For believing in me and giving this a shot.

To Jeanann, I still think version thirty was best. I am forever appreciative of your raw honesty, your bold unwavering peaceful nurture, and the way you rose to challenge me. Never have I needed that more.

To those I have lost, who may still or may no longer walk this Earth, thank you for sharing time when you did and teaching me so much in those moments that stories became necessary to preserve the beauty. I loved you once, its likely I still do.

To Tim, my first fan, none of this could have gotten started without you. All the pages I have yet to fill were first ours. Thanks for allowing our story to exist in a time when it was needed and for helping me raise our beautiful Baby Poet. I am forever in gratitude for that chapter.

& to you, sweet human reader, for giving my book a chance to be on your shelf. That is not something I take lightly and the thought of you reading and sharing my poems with those around you? My eyes will never lose their misty drip.

My favorite quote growing up was in The Things They Carried by Tim O'Brien -

For a few seconds, she was quiet. "Well, right now," she said, "I'm not dead. But when I am, it's like... I don't know, I guess it's like being inside a book that nobody's reading." "A book?" I said. "An old one. It's up on a library shelf, so you're safe and everything, but the book hasn't been checked out for a long, long time. All you can do is wait. Just hope somebody'll pick it up and start reading."

Thank you for reading.

About the Author

Bree Bailey (she/her) is a giggly Latine poet who lives in Southern Austin, TX with her tiny delightful family. As a mental health advocate, Bree speaks openly about her experiences with PTSD, depression and anxiety, while also doing her best to bask in the light and grace of the world. Bree's poems have been featured in *Olney Magazine, Serotonin, Wrongdoing Magazine, West Trade Review, Gulf Stream Magazine,* among others. Most recently, Bree won the 2023 Write Bloody Jack McCarthy National Book Prize and her debut poetry collection, *Wailing on Whisper Street*, now available for purchase with Write Bloody Publishing. Follow her on Instagram @breebaileypoetry or visit her at www.breebaileypoetry.com.

If You Like Bree Bailey, Bree Likes...

A Constellation of Half-Lives
Seema Reza

Cut to Bloom
Noah Arhm Choi

Drive Here and Devastate Me
Megan Falley

Open Your Mouth Like a Bell
Mindy Nettifee

New Shoes on a Dead Horse
Sierra DeMulder

Write Bloody Books

After the Witch Hunt — Megan Falley
Aim for the Head: An Anthology of Zombie Poetry — Rob Sturma, Editor
Allow The Light: The Lost Poems of Jack McCarthy — Jessica Lohafer, Editor
Amulet — Jason Bayani
Any Psalm You Want — Khary Jackson
Atrophy — Jackson Burgess
Birthday Girl with Possum — Brendan Constantine
The Bones Below — Sierra DeMulder
Born in the Year of the Butterfly Knife — Derrick C. Brown
Bouquet of Red Flags — Taylor Mali
Bring Down the Chandeliers — Tara Hardy
Ceremony for the Choking Ghost — Karen Finneyfrock
A Constellation of Half-Lives — Seema Reza
Counting Descent — Clint Smith
Courage: Daring Poems for Gutsy Girls — Karen Finneyfrock, Mindy Nettifee, & Rachel McKibbens, Editors
Cut to Bloom — Arhm Choi Wild
Dear Future Boyfriend — Cristin O'Keefe Aptowicz
Do Not Bring Him Water — Caitlin Scarano
Don't Smell the Floss — Matty Byloos
Drive Here and Devastate Me — Megan Falley
Drunks and Other Poems of Recovery — Jack McCarthy
The Elephant Engine High Dive Revival — Derrick C. Brown, Editor
Every Little Vanishing — Sheleen McElhinney
Everyone I Love Is a Stranger to Someone — Annelyse Gelman
Everything Is Everything — Cristin O'Keefe Aptowicz
Favorite Daughter — Nancy Huang
The Feather Room — Anis Mojgani
Floating, Brilliant, Gone — Franny Choi
Glitter in the Blood: A Poet's Manifesto for Better, Braver Writing — Mindy Nettifee
Gold That Frames the Mirror — Brandon Melendez

The Heart of a Comet — Pages D. Matam

Heavy Lead Birdsong — Ryler Dustin

Heirloom — Ashia Ajani

Here I Am Burn Me — Kimbelry Nguyen

Her Whole Bright Life — Courtney Leblanc

Hello. It Doesn't Matter. — Derrick C. Brown

Help in the Dark Season — Jacqueline Suskin

Hot Teen Slut — Cristin O'Keefe Aptowicz

How the Body Works the Dark — Derrick C. Brown

How to Love the Empty Air — Cristin O'Keefe Aptowicz

I Love Science! — Shanny Jean Maney

I Love You Is Back — Derrick C. Brown

The Importance of Being Ernest — Ernest Cline

The Incredible Sestina Anthology — Daniel Nester, Editor

In Search of Midnight — Mike McGee

In the Pockets of Small Gods — Anis Mojgani

Junkyard Ghost Revival — Derrick C. Brown, Editor

Keep Your Little Lights Alive —John-Francis Quiñonez

Kissing Oscar Wilde — Jade Sylvan

The Last American Valentine — Derrick C. Brown, Editor

The Last Time as We Are — Taylor Mali

Learn Then Burn — Tim Stafford & Derrick C. Brown, Editors

Learn Then Burn Teacher's Guide — Tim Stafford & Molly Meacham, Editors

Learn Then Burn 2: This Time It's Personal — Tim Stafford, Editor

Lessons on Being Tenderheaded — Janae Johnson

Love Ends In A Tandem Kayak — Derrick C. Brown

Love in a Time of Robot Apocalypse — David Perez

The Madness Vase — Andrea Gibson

Multiverse: An Anthology of Superhero Poetry of Superhuman Proportions —
Rob Sturma & Ryk McIntyre, Editors

My, My, My, My, My — Tara Hardy

The New Clean — Jon Sands

New Shoes on a Dead Horse — Sierra DeMulder

Open Your Mouth like a Bell — Mindy Nettifee

Ordinary Cruelty — Amber Flame

Our Poison Horse — Derrick C. Brown

Over the Anvil We Stretch — Anis Mojgani

Pansy — Andrea Gibson

Pecking Order — Nicole Homer

The Pocketknife Bible — Anis Mojgani

Pole Dancing to Gospel Hymns — Andrea Gibson

Racing Hummingbirds — Jeanann Verlee

Reasons to Leave the Slaughter — Ben Clark

Redhead and the Slaughter King — Megan Falley

Rise of the Trust Fall — Mindy Nettifee

Said the Manic to the Muse — Jeanann Verlee

Scandalabra — Derrick C. Brown

Slow Dance with Sasquatch — Jeremy Radin

The Smell of Good Mud — Lauren Zuniga

Some of the Children Were Listening — Lauren Sanderson

Songs from Under the River — Anis Mojgani

Strange Light — Derrick C. Brown

The Tigers, They Let Me — Anis Mojgani

Thin Ice Olympics — Jeffery McDaniel

38 Bar Blues — C.R. Avery

This Way to the Sugar — Hieu Minh Nguyen

Time Bomb Snooze Alarm — Bucky Sinister

Uh-Oh — Derrick C. Brown

Uncontrolled Experiments in Freedom — Brian S. Ellis

The Undisputed Greatest Writer of All Time — Beau Sia

The Way We Move Through Water — Lino Anunciacion

We Will Be Shelter — Andrea Gibson, Editor

What Learning Leaves — Taylor Mali

What the Night Demands — Miles Walser

Working Class Represent — Cristin O'Keefe Aptowicz

Workin' Mime to Five — Dick Richards

Printed in the USA
CPSIA information can be obtained
at www.ICGtesting.com
JSHW080047130424
61107JS00004B/11